MW01531195

LOOK WHERE HE BROUGHT ME FROM

LOOK WHERE HE BROUGHT ME FROM

The Life and Times of Bishop Walter Lewis McBride

BISHOP WALTER L. MCBRIDE

authorHOUSE®

AuthorHouse™
1663 Liberty Drive
Bloomington, IN 47403
www.authorhouse.com
Phone: 1-800-839-8640

© 2011 by Bishop Walter L. McBride. All rights reserved.

No part of this book may be reproduced, stored in a retrieval system, or transmitted by any means without the written permission of the author.

First published by AuthorHouse   11/04/2011

ISBN: 978-1-4670-7306-6 (sc)
ISBN: 978-1-4670-7307-3 (ebk)

Library of Congress Control Number: 2011919147

Printed in the United States of America

Any people depicted in stock imagery provided by Thinkstock are models, and such images are being used for illustrative purposes only.
Certain stock imagery © Thinkstock.

This book is printed on acid-free paper.

Because of the dynamic nature of the Internet, any web addresses or links contained in this book may have changed since publication and may no longer be valid. The views expressed in this work are solely those of the author and do not necessarily reflect the views of the publisher, and the publisher hereby disclaims any responsibility for them.

CONTENTS

Bishop Walter L. McBride
and the late
Sister Lizzie Embary Smith McBride

DEDICATION

This book is dedicated to my wife of sixty years, Lizzie Embary Smith McBride (May 20, 1925-November 1, 2004). She was a faithful wife who was concerned about me completing this book. Lizzie was a great woman of God who stood by me all through the years of my early ministry and made sacrifices right along with me, seeing about the church and taking care of our family. Lizzie traveled with me to most of the foreign countries and within the United States. Whatever needs I had, she was always there to help me. I will always remember the sacrifices she made and dedication she showed during her lifetime. Lizzie was a loyal companion who showed interest in my work. I did a lot of the things and went a lot places because she encouraged me to do so. She never complained about helping me, even though many of her things had to be stopped in order to help me. Lizzie was a woman of great wisdom who gave of herself for family and others. She felt that this book would be a help to those who have a vision, and it would provide knowledge for the days ahead. Lizzie was great at helping me to remember things. I thank God for the steadfastness, dependability, faithfulness, dedication, and the wonderful sixty years He blessed our lives as husband and wife, and for our eight children-Lewis, Charleen, Tillmon, Shirley, Clara, Michael, Ralph, and Chiquita. Lizzie loved her children and grandchildren, and she is greatly missed!

If you remain faithful to God, He will shower blessings upon your lives. It is my prayer that you will find answers, wisdom, and knowledge as you read this book. God bless!

Bishop Walter L. McBride

FOREWORD

Bishop Walter McBride is one of the foremost Bible-knowledgeable men within the Pentecostal Churches of the Apostolic Faith, Inc. (PCAF). He has served in the Southeastern District Council in various capacities for over forty years and has been a stalwart for the Board of Bishops and the Board of Directors for many years, helping to guide the PCAF organization into becoming a viable organization both nationally and internationally.

As one of the senior ministers within the PCAF, he has been an example to the younger ministers, stirring them to study the

Bible. Often he showed them his vast knowledge of the Bible, calling out chapter and verse as he taught in churches within the PCAF and in Apostolic churches throughout the world.

He befriended younger ministers, giving them opportunities to minister to his congregation; men who have become leaders in the Apostolic church such as Bishop John T. Leslie Jr., Bishop Lambert W. Gates Sr., and even me. (I have preached for Bishop McBride for over thirty-five years, sometimes twice a year in one of his churches.)

Bishop McBride is a strong pastoral leader, overseeing as many as five churches that were directly under his pastoral ministry. He served the Henry church in Tennessee (Henry Pentecostal Church) for over forty years and was one of the charter members of the church in Medon, Tennessee (Whitehall Church of God) which has been in existence for over fifty years.

He fulfills the Scripture as a bishop, showing himself to be full of hospitality, very capable in teaching, and an Apostolic preacher standing among the best (1 Timothy 3:2). To know Bishop McBride is to sit and enjoy the wonderful wisdom he possesses and the experience he has encountered as an Apostolic Pentecostal minister. He is a man of integrity who does not try to deceive but speaks the truth and lies not.

One of my most memorable activities with Bishop Walter McBride was when we were traveling together to go preach at the Henry Church in Tennessee. That night, he delivered a calf. It was truly an unforgettable experience!

It is my belief that anyone reading this book will discover valuable insight. Without hesitation, I wholeheartedly recommend it to you. This is a book about a man who has made history and will leave a legacy and example for men and women to follow.

Bishop J. E. Moore
Presiding Prelate
Pentecostal Churches of the Apostolic Faith, Inc.

ACKNOWLEDGMENTS

The following individuals were instrumental in making this book a reality:

Lizzie Embary Smith McBride for her steadfastness, dependability, faithfulness, dedication, encouragement, and sixty wonderful years of marriage and eight beautiful children.

Shirley A. Collier for your encouragement and support of this book and serving as an advisor.

Mildred D. Pettiford for helping with the myriad details in shaping the content and format of this book.

Bishop J. E. Moore for your valuable time in writing the foreword.

Sister Sandra Hych for the beautiful poem.

CHAPTER ONE

THE FORMATIVE YEARS

This book is about my life and lifestyle as a poor country boy who has been blessed of the Lord, and about my life as a preacher and pastor. I was born May 6, 1926, to Moses Walter and Velma (Croom) McBride, the sixth child of thirteen siblings. Our family was very, very poor. I often think of the many times we would have to walk to school (about two miles) with no shoes, even when the ground was frozen. Upon arriving at school, I would take my hat off and put it on my feet for warmth. I grew up in Marshall Community, a small community in Medon, Tennessee with a population of approximately 150. I was educated to the eighth grade in a community school for the black kids, in Marshall Chapel Church. This was the only school I attended until after the military, when I entered GI school to study agriculture for eighteen months. I could not afford to further my education, because there were no schools for black kids within our community.

Even though we were very poor, at the age of nine I began to think about what I wanted my future to be like, and one thing I wanted was to have something of my own. We had no money, yet I had a purpose in life. I only had one pair of overalls and would wear them for the whole week. On Saturday evenings, we would go to bed early so my mother would be able to wash our clothes so that we would have them to wear to church that Sunday morning. We all had one pair of shoes that would have to last us for a year. I recall the last speech I said at church; the top of my boots were cut off, and my shirt had been made by my mother from a sugar sack. The whiskey makers would give our mom the empty sacks from twenty-pound bags of sugar, and she would make us shirts from those bags.

During the winter months, I would go into the woods to hull walnuts and pick up hickory nuts and things of such to help us survive. After the farmers finished harvesting the corn, I would go into the corn fields to find some ears of corn to bring back home, where they were put on the heater to parch so that we would have food to eat. I recall that at the age of eleven I was thrown by a mule that I was riding, and I broke my left arm. At that time we did not believe in going to a doctor, so Brother Johnny Marshall, the founder of Marshall Community, placed my left arm on a wide board and, hitting it with his hand, put my bone back in place. To this day, I have no problem with that arm. When I was fourteen years old, my father hired me out to a white woman and her son. To this day, I remember that I felt like a slave during that time period. I would have to eat my meals outside because blacks were not allowed to eat in the white folks' house. I worked for them for about three years. During those years, I constantly thought about how I would someday have something of my own.

In 1944, at one time I stayed with my sister Gladys and her children to help her make a cotton crop, because her husband, Milton, was in the army. After helping my sister gather the crop,

I married Lizzie E. Smith. I was eighteen years old, and she was nineteen. Of course, we had liked each other since we were six years old. And our marriage lasted sixty years. As I tell the saints, two of the hardest things in life are staying married and staying saved. After our marriage, my mother gave me a shoulder of meat and a frying pan. Sister Callie Bell Marshall, the woman who raised Lizzie, gave her a skillet. We were married on the twenty-fourth of October, 1944.

I was inducted into the US Army, February 2, 1945, and boy did I do some crying. After returning from the service, Lizzie and I farmed on twenty-one acres of land left to Lizzie and her sisters by their mother, Roseanna (Lee) Marshall. When we went to get married, Uncle John Spencer, Lizzie's great-uncle, took us to Jackson, TN to ride the bus to Corinth, Mississippi. After paying the justice of the peace $4.50, I had $1.50 left. Lizzie and I started from that and worked together and raised a family of eight children.

While we educated our children, my wife worked as a licensed beautician. We farmed, and I also worked as a laborer, helping to build Jackson General Hospital in 1948. From there I went to H. W. Smith Plumbing Company and helped build Parkview and East Chester schools, and from there I went to work for the Illinois Central Railroad for seventeen years until it closed in 1967. During this time, I was still farming and raising cattle and hogs. This was the livelihood of my natural life. We had four boys (Lewis, Tilmon, Michael, and Wayne) and four girls (Charleen, Shirley, Clara, and Chiquita). My wife and I were married sixty years on October 24, 2004. She passed away November 2, 2004. God blessed us with a good life.

Chapter Two

The Spiritual Life

During our childhood, we attended the community church at Marshall Chapel Church of God. We really thought that we were saved until my mother got the revelation of the church as she read the Bible, and God opened her eyes about the Apostolic Doctrine. Oh boy, did that bring about a controversy within the church!

The Whitehall Church of God came into existence September 1953, because some of the saints were convicted that the Apostolic Doctrine was the true plan of salvation. The Marshall Chapel Church of God leaders were not in agreement; therefore, the believing saints were put out of the community church. This was the beginning of Whitehall Church of God. My mother, Velma (Croom) McBride, was studying the Bible and came into the knowledge and conviction of how the early church began. Because of her conviction, she told Elder Johnny Marshall (pastor of the church) that she read in the Bible where the early church started on the day of Pentecost. His comment to her was, "That was for them at that time, and it is not for this day."

But he told her that if that was her conviction, he would take her to Lacy McDaniel's large pond on his farm to be baptized in Jesus's name. This was in 1947, if my memory serves me right. Others who were also baptized in Jesus's name at the same time were my two brothers, Charles and Wilford, my sister Gladys, and Joel March. The other church leaders were not in agreement and put my mother out of the church, and she had nowhere to go to worship. She was disfellowshipped in 1947 and was without a church home until 1949, when the church was reunited briefly. There were about twenty saints who were put out of the church. This was the beginning of Whitehall Church of God.

When Elder Floyd Marshall took charge of the church, there had been conflict over our religious teaching about going into the army. The first group was taught not to go into the army. Several of them did not go and were put in jail. I was the first one to break rank and join the army. After that, one of the church leaders said that Brother Johnny Marshall was wrong for teaching them not to go into the army. Of those who went to prison were my brother, Joe, my brother-in-law, Milton, Lee Reeves, Marshall Thompson, Houston Thompson, C. M. Thompson, Naaman Marshall, David Marshall, and Robert Marshall. All of them went to prison first. However, some of them finally gave in and went into the army. My brother, Joe, did not go. He was paroled out in St. Louis and made that his home, working and raising his family there.

It became a doctrinal issue, and then when different people began to preach, there would be opposing beliefs. Elder Ed Blissett, a native of Arkansas and a preacher who had married Mother Marshall, was convicted that the Apostolic doctrine was right. He stated that he had sixteen people to baptize, but knew that baptizing them in the name of the Father, Son, and Holy Ghost was not according to the Apostles doctrine. Soon afterwards, he began to baptize people (including members of our family) in Jesus's name. This meant that they put us out of Marshall Chapel Church of God, leaving us with no place to worship.

For about one year, we had services in a little brush arbor which we put up. It was made of sticks with poles across the top and some green limbs laid over those for shade. From there we went to a tent. Then we talked to the school superintendent about the old schoolhouse that was located above our current church. We were granted permission to use the building. I took my two oldest boys (Lewis and Tilmon) in a wagon with barrels of water to wash the building down. My father (Moses) and I would wash the building down on Saturdays, then go and have service on Sundays. We would get full of bird lice during the day services, and we would come back home and take our baths and go back to Sunday night service.

Finally I said to my daddy, "Papa, go see Mr. Will Morgan and see if he will sell us some land to build a church." In the community where we lived, the church leaders would laugh and talk and say we wouldn't be able to do anything. They thought we wouldn't be able to build a church, and that we would be coming back to Marshall because we had no other place to go. My brother-in-law, Milton, told them, "Ya'll don't know Walter. If he says something will get done, it will happen." Papa met with Mr. Will Morgan, and he sold us two acres for $50, where the current church is now located. I think Mother Marshall and Sister Mae Spencer gave the first fifty cents, and we raised $250 for our building fund.

Papa and I went to Conger and Parker Lumber Company, which used to be located where the farmers market is now. Bob Conger (former mayor of Jackson, Tennessee) owned the lumber company. They asked us how much money we had; we told them $250. They said, "Bring it up here and get anything you need." The initial building was forty feet by thirty-two feet. Josh Hardin, a white fellow from Toone, Tennessee, laid the concrete blocks. We added expansions in 1956, 1964, 1967, 1977, and 1992. Later, in 2000, we did another addition.

So the Lord has blessed us, even though the naysayers said it couldn't be done. The Lord blessed us to build our church, and that is why I always say that our church was built for the Apostolic Doctrine. All of this came about under my leadership with the help of the Lord. So I am still very much determined to continue right now, and I am glad that the saints stayed with me even in the midst of a lot of false predictions that went out. That did not stop the work of God, because God knew the purpose we were here. Whitehall Church of God is a special place of worship because we were the only blacks who had an Apostolic church anywhere between here and Memphis (and to our knowledge, between here and Nashville, Tennessee). So the church is actually a great landmark for the black community of Medon, Tennessee.

I worked hard within the church, because it hurt my spirit that the so-called saints had put my mom and others out of the church because of the name of Jesus. During those earlier years of the church, I was not a minister. My ministry began in 1955. I felt the calling coming out of Tiptonville, Mississippi, when after feeling the anointing of God, I went into the ministry. As of this writing, I have been in the ministry fifty-five years, and I have done the best that I could afford to do. In 1954 I was baptized in Jesus's name. I felt the call into the ministry in 1955 during a service when something struck me. I had never thought about becoming a pastor. I was faithful and just wanted to be saved and a servant of God.

My first sermon was preached on September 25, 1955; it was the fourth Sunday in September, and I have been busy ever since. In 1956 I was asked to preach at a Baptist church, every first Sunday for one and a half years. God was very good to me. He blessed my ministry very much. I preached at Tiptonville, Cotton Plant, and Sledge, Mississippi. All these places were in my early ministry, as well as Arkansas, Haiti, Missouri, Alabama, California, Illinois, Arizona, Seattle, Washington, Washington D.C., Louisiana, Georgia, Ohio, New York, Kentucky, Michigan, and Florida. At this time I had officiated 87 deaths and 59 weddings. Since that time, the number has risen to 114 deaths and 78 weddings.

These are some historical dates of revivals I have preached at over the years:

1957: Cotton Plant, Mississippi

1958: Cotton Plant and Tiptonville, Mississippi

1959: Sledge, Mississippi; Hayti, Missouri

1960: Arkansas; Hayti, Missouri

1961: St. Louis, Missouri; East St. Louis, Illinois; Arkansas

1968: New York City; Terre Haute, Indiana; Louisville, Kentucky

1975: I went to California and Arizona and preached at nine churches in two weeks. I was with Bishop Stallworth, Elder Hall, and Elder Pottergy, in Stockton, California. Then I joined Bishop Jones in Sacramento, and from there went to Monrovia to be with Pastor Delaney and Bishop Morgan. I returned to Los Angeles to meet with Elder Singleton, and then I traveled to Phoenix, Arizona, to be with Elder Taylor and Elder Young.

CHAPTER THREE

FOREIGN TRAVELS

My travel in foreign countries began in 1970. I ran a revival for Elder Finley, in Decauter, Alabama, came home for two days, and then left for a two-week trip that began in Belfast, Ireland. With me were Bishop Robert L. Little and his wife; Brother Raulf (from South Bend, Indiana); a brother from Evansville, Indiana; Brother White from Ohio, and others. We went for the 1970 Apostolic World Christian Fellowship meeting in Belfast, Ireland. During that time, the president of France had passed away. We returned to London, England, and visited the Church of England where I stood over the graves of those who died for religious freedom.

It was amazing crossing the Irish Sea—we went across on a big, fine ship. What was amazing to me was that when I went to Ireland, and they called out my name, "Brother McBride," the Irish people got excited and started cheering like they were at a ball game. It frightened me because I had found out that there was a religious war going on between the Protestants and Catholics for twelve hundred years, with each side trying to get control so it could rule the other. They said to me, "He is of us, he's of us," which made me very afraid. So there I found out that the origin of the McBride name is Irish. I did not know that, because being uneducated, I didn't know who I was. And we as

African Americans don't know who we are anyway, having been sold from one slave master to another and given the name of the slave owners.

I also visited Scotland, France, and England. We went across to Dover, England, to Calais, France, the day President Charles de Gaulle was buried. Everything was closed except restaurants. None of us could speak French, and the Frenchmen couldn't speak English. Bishop Robert Little knew how to say "bean soup" in French, and we all had to eat bean soup. It was served with a big bowl of water and a big, hard bun.

My next foreign trip was to Israel in 1972, and I remember that we flew on a big plane with five hundred passengers. While in Israel, we had Communion in little wooden cups. I have some at home now that were brought back when my wife and I returned to Israel in 1977. Bishop Moore, Bishop Wright, Jerry Jones, Bishop Bell, and others went with us. We went on to Egypt—my first time being there. We went up on Mt. Zion where Moses received the law. The Lord blessed all of us who went. We rode a camel part of the way (paying twelve dollars apiece), but we didn't go far. The camel didn't go far because we were going on to Mt. Zion. I did not know if I would ever get back or not, because every six or seven steps I would be out of breath. I asked the Lord, "Please don't let me die in Egypt," and of course, this will not be a problem—that was my first and last trip to Egypt.

I visited Israel, Jericho, Bethlehem, Palestine, and so many other places that I can't recall them all by name. Also on that trip, we went to Paris, France; England; and Rome, Italy. In 1977,

I returned to Israel and went the same route: Rome, Italy; Paris, France; and other countries. I took my last trip to Israel in 1996, the year my mother passed away. In my church office I have the pictures of where we were in Jerusalem; I was on a camel, and my mother was standing beside the camel.

Beginning in 1979, I visited Haiti three times 1979, 1980, and 1982. During those years, I was preaching for Suffragan Bishop John H. Pettiford every other year, mostly in St. Louis, Missouri. Even though I did a lot of traveling overseas, I was still taking care of my church work back in the States.

Chapter Four

Pastoral Responsibilities

I was elected pastor for Decatur, Alabama, which meant that I was responsible for other churches in Butler, Alabama; Columbia, Tennessee; and Hollis Spring, Mississippi. In 1976, I went to Elder Parnell; then in April, to Elder J. E. Moore, Joliet, Illinois, and to Bishop Young, Cincinnati, Ohio; in June, to Elder Fred Donahue, Gary, Indiana; in July, to Elder Osborn Mosley, Americus, Georgia; in August, to Elder Neely Dotson, Chicago, IL. Continuing my travels in 1977, I went to Bishop Young in April; in June, to Elder John H. Pettiford Sr., East St. Louis, Illinois; in July, to Elder Mosley again, Americus, Georgia; and in August, to Elder Neely Dotson. I began 1978 by visiting Elder J. E. Moore in March; then in April I went to Bishop Young, Cincinnati, OH; in August, to Elder Neely Dotson, Chicago, IL; in October, Elder Sam Jones, back in Sacramento, CA. I saw Elder Neely Dotson again in Chicago in 1979; then Elder Sam Jones in October, and Elder J. E. Moore in December. My schedule in 1982 included Bishop Young in April; in May, Elder Moore; in June, Bishop Little; in August, Elder Dotson; and Bishop James A. Johnson, St. Louis, Missouri; and in November, Elder Pettiford. In 1983 I preached mostly on the West Coast.

As you can see, I had a very busy schedule down through the years. I was preaching in Cotton Plant, Mississippi, when I heard about the saints in Henry, Tennessee. They came to us, and they kept on coming every year. They would attend the church councils. Finally, I was elected to pastor the church in Henry, Tennessee. I pastored that church for forty four years. When I gave it up, the members had the opportunity to select whomever they wanted for a pastor. I did not influence their selection. I had served them very well during those years. God has blessed me, and as this book is being made, I am hoping my future will be better. I am now taking the position as a senior pastor and am determined to stay in the Apostolic doctrine. I have had a lot of good days and bad days, but my good days outweigh my bad ones. I have experienced many disruptions within the church life. Yet the Lord kept me encouraged to keep the faith and to hold on to the Word of God. I don't know how long I will be in the land of the living, but I am still encouraged.

I want to talk about the church and what has happened over the years under my leadership. First I would like to go back to the church I helped to build in Brownsville, Tennessee, where Sister Byron was pastor. Here is a report of the church at home after the building of our church in 1956. We did more remodeling in 1964 and 1967, and then in 1977 and 1992 we did additions. At Henry, we remodeled four times under my leadership.

Confucius wrote: "A superior man has nine aims: to see clearly, to understand what he hears, to be warm in manner, dignified in bearing, faithful in speech, painstaking at work, to ask when in doubt, in anger to think of difficulties, in sight of gain to remember what's right. Something we must consider, if there be any righteousness in heart, there will be beauty in character. If there be beauty in character, there will be harmony in the home. If there be harmony in the home, there will be order in the nation. If there will be order in the nation, there will be peace in the world."

Those are the nine aims for a superior man. I have tried to be a man of understanding. I am very concerned about the future of our world and what it is going to accomplish. Every person should strive to seek the will of God. God has tremendously blessed me, and I have had a lot of experience being a little country boy. I didn't know if I would ever be privileged to have had such a great experience, and I don't know if I will ever get through telling all I have been through. But God has blessed me so far to enjoy my latest years. As I already stated, I try to let my last days be my best days. The song "Down Through the Years the Lord's Been Good To Me" is a testament of my life.

Chapter Five

Life Reflections-The Interview

Q1: Bishop McBride, you mention that you had been to GI school. What basically did you study during that time?

A1: I studied agriculture, fruit trees, and how to keep a record of your crops, budgeting, how much money you spend, learning the business of farming, different types of seeds, and the time to grow crops. I also raised cattle, and that was the most important part of farming.

Q2: Would you say that going to GI school is what gave you the sense of how to take care of business, given the limited amount of money you have had, and looking at what you have accomplished?

A2: Yes. It taught me how to govern myself and how that the greatest part of management was completing a project.

Q3: You mentioned that you had broken one of your arms. Which one was it, and how was it taken care of?

A3: After being thrown by a mule, my left arm was hanging down. They carried me to the house of our pastor, Elder Johnny

Marshall, who held it down real tight, wrapped it on a wide board, hit it, and set it back in place.

Q4: What do you think made the people in that day think it was a sin to go to the doctor?

A4: Religious conviction. Religion has done more damage to man than good, because religion is a thing that gives you a feeling not a conviction. If it can convince you that what you are doing is right, you'll die for religion's sake. The old saints probably would have lived ten to fifteen years longer for just little minor things, but they would not go to a doctor to be seen and treated. Back in those days, you weren't allowed to go to the doctor. If your wife was in labor during childbirth and was having a hard time, they would go into the field and get the men to come and hold her on the bed (I'm telling the truth!). She would have to have the baby or die. Your mommy's great aunt, Sister Lou, died giving birth right across the road over there [pointing in the direction where the house was at that time.] If we felt sick—you know sometimes you felt bad and did not feel like going to church—or if you did not call for the elders of the church or if you didn't come to church, it was considered sinning. I guess that is why I felt such an unction to preach. They were so unbalanced. Religion will make a fool out of you.

Q5: I know we have heard over the years of instances where people would have that real strong faith. Can you name or talk about some of the instances that the faith was portrayed when you were growing up?

A5: My daddy had a sore throat (they called it a sore throat), but it was strep throat. His neck bulged out and burst on the outside. When he would drink water, it would drain on the outside of his neck until it healed back up. I saw that with my own eyes.

Q6: And he lived to be what age?

A6: He lived to be eighty-three years old.

Q7: What age was he when that situation happened?

A7: He was somewhere in his late fifties. So he lived thirty something years after that. I have seen so much. I have seen people right at the point of death, and then they get up—and then I have seen those that didn't get up.

Q8: What age were you when you preached your first sermon, and do you recall the title?

A8: Yes, I was twenty nine years old when I preached my first sermon. The title was [I think] "Laying up in store a foundation for the life to come that you might lay hold unto eternal life," taken from I Timothy 6:19.

Q9: We know you have a gift of having a photographic memory where you can just quote Scriptures. How would you describe the ability to do that?

A9: That is real plain to me. In the car, I was coming back from Tiptonville, Mississippi. Tilmon [my second-oldest son] was about seven years old. He had gone down there with me that night. I wasn't preaching then, but on my way back there was a real heaviness, just like a weight on me to preach. No voice, I did not hear a voice—just a weight. It was because I hadn't gotten over how they did my mother and the others after their baptism in Jesus's name. Because they were saying they were sanctified, I grew up down there, and all they taught was that ain't nobody right but us. When mommy got the knowledge of the Scriptures of when the church started [see mommy would read the Old and New Testaments], she told Brother Johnny [Big Momma's husband], "I see where the church started on the day of Pentecost." Brother Johnny said to mommy, "Sister Velma, that wasn't to us." He and another elder both said, "Naw, that ain't for our day."

So, mommy didn't say no more about her spiritual conviction until later. So Brother Johnny went back (he was pretty zealous), and he asked Momma, "Sister Velma, you say the Lord told you?" She said, "I did not tell you the Lord told me, I said I read it." He said, "Well, all right. If you think that's it, I will carry you over there to Brother Tout Daniels (a white brother), and you can get baptized." Brother Johnny wouldn't have put her out of the church, but the assistant pastor and some of the church members had been split over going to the army. Well, Brother Johnny did not want to do nothing else to cause another split in the church. The assistant pastor is the one that wanted Mommy disfellowshipped. He said, "Well, you need to disfellowship Sister Velma, she don't need to be with us, because the Bible ought to speak the same thing."

See, you can be dumb and not even know how dumb you really are. The assistant pastor was 95 percent infidel anyway. He thought more of the churches that did not profess holiness. See, Marshall Chapel was supposed to be a sanctified church, and the other was a Methodist Church. I knew a time when the Methodists and Baptists themselves didn't fellowship together. They mix with everyone now. That's why they are changing to all these different names like Christ's Ministries and things like that. They don't have the true doctrine. The Scripture Acts 2:42 says, "And they continued steadfastly in the apostles' doctrine" and fellowship, and in breaking of bread, and in prayers.(KJV). They just all worship together.

After Lizzie and I married, we went back to the church down there and then Lizzie was the last one that got baptized in Jesus's name. Catherine, Willie Mae, all of them got baptized, in Jesus's name. They didn't put no pressure on them. Lizzie was milking the cow one day, and she said the felt a heaviness on her. It was like she heard a voice saying, "The baptism in Jesus's name is right." And so many of us got baptized at that time. The assistant pastor called a meeting and put us all out of the church. He said, "I don't want you all in here worshipping with us, and we won't worship with you all." So that's where it started. We didn't have anywhere to go for church services. So they started laughing and saying, "Aw, they'll soon be back; they ain't got nowhere to go."

But we started out at the old brush hog with the sticks sticking up. Then we put tree limbs on top of it for shade. We didn't stay in there too long. We had a tent and went down there where Blairs Chapel is and started having service. Elder Neal finally came with us, then Papa. Papa didn't come with us at first. So they came, and we got that old schoolhouse that used to be above our current church where John Albert Merriweather lived. That's where my mommy used to go to school. Aunt Nan McBride, was the one that taught school. That was before my day.

But anyway, when I got baptized, and was filled with the Holy Ghost, we all left Marshall Chapel. I told Papa (my dad), "Papa, you go see Mr. William Morgan and see if he will sell us some ground." I have always been a mystery to these people in this community, now you think about it—a nineteen-year-old boy building him a house. That's something, that's very rare, a person nineteen years old. Even some of the grown men around here didn't have nothing. So they laughed and said, "They ain't going to do nothing." Floyd and Elmer Marshall across the road there, said, "They can't build no church." Milton told them, "Ya'll don't know Walter."

Shucks, Papa and I started out finding what would it take for us to build a church. Sister Mae Spencer (Big Momma) gave the first fifty cents. We just started a little treasury before we even found anywhere to build a church. We had about fifty dollars in the treasury. So we went to the Morgan and Parker Lumber Company. [Where the farmers market is now it used to be a big lumberyard, and William Morgan owned it]. We carried him $200 for the land, and where the church is setting now was nothing but trees. We cut them down low, and the bulldozer pushed it down.

Q10: What year did they split the church?

A10: It was 1953. Well, actually the first time it split it was in 1943. The brothers that refused to go to the army had gone to prison. The war was going on, and I was eighteen years old in 1944. The church had split in 1943 because Brother Johnny was in the penitentiary when I asked for Lizzie Embary. I was talking to her about marriage, and she said, "Well, let me make up my mind." That's what she said.

So it was in May of 1944 when she said yes she would marry me. So we planned to marry that October. I asked Big Momma about marrying her. She stood there for a while—she was cutting some bushes—and she looked at me and said, "Yes, now if you are not going to treat her right, bring her back home." And so October 24, 1944, Lizzie and I married. Then I went into the army, and when I went into the army, Arthur Lee was about four years old, I guess. I went in the army that January and came out that May. The war had ceased; the Germans had surrendered. The day the Germans surrendered, I finished my basic training.

And Arthur Lee, I guess, dreamed it; he told Mommy, "Uncle Walter is coming home next week." And they said, "Arthur Lee, where you get that at?" He said, "That's all right." I didn't tell nobody. I walked in and they had a "fit".

I got here in time enough then to make a crop. We were living across the road there where those girls are living now—a little old log house. That's where we were at before I left. But that was when I was telling about when I went down to Toone and bought a brand-new wagon on credit, a mule wagon. Just my word, and I paid him that fall. And I have been going ever since. But now in the ministry, that's what you were asking me about—early ministry. After I started in the ministry, I was working on the railroad, and a fellow named Simpson had a son-in-law named J. W. Jones. That's the guy, that I was telling you about who called me, and asked me to send him $200 to Atlanta, Georgia. He did not tell me what he wanted if for. I didn't really know the fellow.

Simpson's mother-in-law had gone to Ohio somewhere and went to an Apostolic Church and got baptized in Jesus's name. I didn't know her then. But, after she came back down to Grand Junction, she was telling folks about the baptism in Jesus's name. It stirred the people up, and all that was new and everything. So Simpson asked me, "Say Mac [that's what they called me], will you come down and preach for us if I can get you an appointment?" I said, "Ya, I can come down and preach for you."

I preached to that Baptist congregation every first Sunday for eighteen months. That was 1956 to some parts of 1958, and they didn't turn me out, I quit 'cause everybody left. There was a little bright, nice-looking young lady who got up one time and said, "Ya'll running around here talking about ya'll wanted what was right. Reverend McBride been down here preaching for a long time and ain't none of ya'll done nothing, ain't a thing to none of you." [He laughs as he remembers this incident.] She told them that. When I first started preaching, the house was full; when I stopped, it was empty. Nobody ever got baptized down there, nobody. See, that was a learning experience for me that you don't play with religion; religion is powerful.

I preached my first sermon at Whitehall Church of God the fifth Sunday in September 1956. I wasn't preaching long before I went down there to preach at the Baptist church. Then at nineteen I was going to a lot of different churches, and folks were calling me and then they asked me to come to Cotton Plant and pastor a church while I was Brother James Thompson's assistant pastor.

They wanted me to be the pastor, but I never accepted the pastorate in Cotton Plant, Mississippi. But I preached down there every third Sunday. That's how I got to Henry, TN. Henry heard about us. Sister Sadie Harris, would run up and down the road going to different churches anyhow. She heard about Henry, so she went to Henry. She and Sister Elsie used to fellowship with the Church of God in Christ here in Jackson, TN. She hadn't seen Sister Anderson in so long, so they didn't know each other too well. They went to one another and the one said, "Is this Sister Anderson?" She said, "Yeah, this is Sister Harris." So that's what started the relationship with the saints in Henry, TN.

So Sister Anderson told her, "Well, I know who Jesus is." "You do?" That's what Sister Harris said. "If you do, you better do something." So they asked for the directions to come to our church. So they came, and I wasn't there. After they came, my sister Gladys said, (that was in 1960), "Boy you ought to have been here today." I was down in Cotton Plant then. She said, "Some people come here today from Henry, TN." I said, "Where is Henry, TN?" She said, "I don't know." See, I had never heard of Henry. I had been working on the railroad up there in Milan, but I had never heard of Henry. I had heard of Atwood, McKenzie, Trezevant, Paris, but I had never heard of Henry. She said, "I don't know where it's at." Anyhow, they came that Sunday. Remember Brother Miller? He was on fire you know. Brother James Thompson told me, "Brother Walter, those saints from Henry is coming back, and I would like for you to be here. I think they're going to come down here to get baptized."

So that Saturday, they came down and we met them up in Jackson. T. D. and I, met them at Wortham Church. Wortham had a church there in Jackson. He let us use his pool. I baptized twelve, T. D., Sister Anderson, and I was the first one in the water, then Brother Porter, and all the rest—it was twelve. The next Saturday they came, we baptized eight, that was twenty in all. Then that following Sunday I went up there, we baptized four more, then it was twenty-six members. I baptized twenty-four of them, when I started, and I stayed there forty-four years.

We first started having services in the schoolhouse there in Henry. The people went to the superintendent and said, "We ain't going to have that racket up here," so we left there and went to Sister Anderson's house. The people said we were keeping up too much racket, so we went on out to Brother Porter's place. I told Sister Anderson, "You all go borrow some money. We will build a church." We were carried to court by the Church of God in Christ organization. The judge didn't tell us not to go back to the church; he said to let the church stay in the name that it was (Church of God in Christ).

Of course, it didn't matter to us. The pastor at that time was Buford McTizic. But we left that church and had service at Brother Porter's until we built that church. We left that old church and built a new church. We left there in January, and in June, we had the new church where it is now. They borrowed $800 and we went from there. Built the kitchen after that and fixed it up from there. I tell you, telling my life story is something else.

Q11: Who would you say has been the pastor or person that had the greatest influence on your spiritual growth?

A11: District Elder Hogan and District Elder John H. Pettiford Sr. Those two. See, I could have been in the Pentecostal Assemblies of the World (P.A. of W., Inc.). That's the reason I say that sometimes an organization can hurt you and do you more harm than good. Now, the Midwestern Council was up there in St. Louis and they wouldn't have nothing to do with us down here. You could fellowship together, but couldn't be a member of the Council living in Tennessee. I was in St. Louis visiting and I preached at the Council. Bishop James A. Johnson then was the general secretary and the late Bishop P. L. Scott was the diocesan over the Council. See, neither one of them had been elevated to the bishopric at that time.

Bishop Johnson always wanted me to be in that organization, and they were talking to me about it and I said yes, because Dawson and I preached together a lot. Dawson was in Clarksdale, Mississippi when he said, "Elder McBride, let's go and get in an organization." He [Dawson] had been in the P. A. of W. but he got out. He wanted to start something of his own anyway, and he thought I was going to go with him. We went to Terre Haute, Indiana and when we came back, he decided he was going to start an organization.

So I went on to get in the P. A. of W. organization in St. Louis. I had everything ready—my card, my money, my license, and all. When they brought it to the late Bishop Austin A. Layne, he turned it down. He said, "Now, you all know I love Elder McBride, but if we let him come up here in this Midwestern Council, now, we can do it, but when we get to the National Convention, it will be a floor fight." Now, you know I had these two churches; it would have been something bringing two churches in, but they turned me down.

By that time, Bishop Robert Little came through Tennessee, he had heard about me from Joe Topkins, of Milwaukee, Wisconsin. Lizzie Embary and I had been to Detroit, MI and we were on our way back home. We were riding on the train and we changed trains in Chicago, IL. When we got on the train, Joe Topkins was sitting in there—a little black fellow with a hat on.

He was reading, so I spoke to him. Lizzie Embary went on to her coach, and I went to the rest room.

So when I came back, I asked him, "Are you a minister?" He said, "Yes, yes I am." I said, "What kind?" He said, "Apostolic." I said, "That's what I am." He said, "It is? Who are you?" I said, "McBride." He said, "Oh, yeah. I am Joe Topkins and I am on my way to Jackson, Tennessee. I have never been there and don't know anybody there." I said, "Yeah, that's my home." He said, "It is?" I said, "What are you on your way there for?" He said, "I got a corpse on the train. I am going to bury a lady in Jackson, Tennessee."

I knew he was from Milwaukee. I said, "Uh, what's her name?" He said, "Emma Sykes." I said, "She used to be a member of my church." He said, "What did you say your name was?" I said, "Walter McBride." He said, "I heard her talk about you. Yea, I got to meet a lady down there named Sister Sadie Harris." I said, "She is a member of my church now." He said, "She is?" I said, "I can't go to this funeral, me and Dawson was preaching, I am just on my way home from Detroit, but some of the members will be there, and they can bring you out to my church." So he preached, Joe could preach at that time, so that's how we met. Then I cut loose from Dawson; we didn't have a falling out or anything I was just so busy. Of course, Dawson wanted his own organization. So that's the way it was.

Q12: So did Bishop Little bring you into the Pentecostal Churches of the Apostolic Faith, Inc. (PCAF)? A12: Yes, Little brought me into the PCAF. I joined them in 1964.

Q13: You mentioned the various churches you pastored. How long did you pastor each one?

A13: Butler, Alabama—I didn't stay there long. I gave it over to Genie Sheriff. Nemiah Smith was the one that wanted me to take it over. I didn't know the folks. Nemiah was in Detroit, but he had preached down there and asked me if I would go down there and pastor it, so I did and after a short time I gave it to Sheriff.

Then Decatur, Alabama selected me as their pastor. I already had Henry and Whitehall, but Elder Hogan told them to get me. Strong—he just died here a few months ago—they sent him out of Birmingham, Alabama to take the Decatur church. See, that was Elder Hogan's church. Elder Hogan got to the place where he had gotten old and he didn't want to pastor anymore. He stayed gone all the time anyhow. So it didn't make no difference. When Strong came to them he said, "All you old folks ought to be dead, including District Elder Hogan." "What did he say that for?" those folks said. "We ain't going to have you; we will leave this organization."

Elder Hogan told Bishop Charles Lee—he was in some parts of Ohio—he told him, "Bishop Lee, you better move that little fellow (talking about Strong) back because these folks ain't going to have him." "They're going to keep him," says Bishop Lee. So the church told Elder Hogan, "We are going to leave this organization. Tell us somebody to go to." He said, "Get Elder McBride." I already had Henry and Whitehall then, I had already given up Butler, Alabama. So they called me. Deacon Roberton thought Elder Hogan said my name was Medon. He said, "We want to speak to Elder Medon." [He laughs.] I said, "This is McBride. Who is this?" He said, "Elder Hogan told us to call you. We want you to come down and be our pastor."

I went down. I was about forty something, so they selected me as their pastor. Chiquita [she was two years old], Wayne, Michael, and I [he laughs] went down there. I had been preaching then twenty-five years. So they bought Lizzie Embary a purse. I stayed there for about six months. I would go there once a month. And I told them, "This is too much for me." I told Little, "They could have that church, because that was my church."

Then I was over Columbia, Tennessee. I didn't stay there long. I turned it over to that man—what was his name, oh I can't think of it now—but Chris went down there to preach. Then Hollis Spring, that was my church. One of his preachers from John H. Pettiford's church had gone down there; he's back with John now I guess. But anyway, John called me, and had me to get Steve up there at Lane College. So I went down to Hollis Spring. Some loafer was down there to run a revival. He would get through with one week and say the Lord told me to run another week. So they told me to come down there. When I went down there and that bugger left and got out of there—he never did come in the house. I never did see him. So I had that church and I gave it to Mario Price. And Mario didn't keep it, and then after he left, we let Sean Robertson have it. Mario would go back down there at times to visit, I don't know why he did not keep the church. I thought that was pretty foolish.

Q14: I know you have had a lot of experience with different spirits in the church, so what advice would you have for a young minister in dealing with people in that type of situation?

A14: Any preacher, who is going to do the work of God, he or she needs to stay in the Scripture—don't come up with nothing God told him; stay in the Scriptures. Even if you have an unction and you feel like it's God in it, if you don't have scriptural proof of the individual that that's the work of God, you let that alone. I woke up this morning and the Scripture Isaiah 61 was running through my mind.

Even Jesus took the Scriptures. Jeus, when His ministry time came, went right into the synagogue and they gave Him the book. That was Isaiah 61; He took that and preached to the people. You don't get a lot of doctrine in Matthew, Mark, and Luke—no more than He's talking to the Jews. John tells about Him in the Scriptures of St. John. Jesus would talk to them about what the Scriptures said. If any man believes on me as the Scriptures has said, out of his belly will flow rivers of living waters. [St. John 7:37-38]. So to the ministers: you do like the Scriptures say. He (Jesus) was the Scripture Himself in a human body.

But what's in the world today is spirits; people don't pay no attention to that Bible. And that's the only spiritual direction we got. That's the reason John told them don't believe every spirit; it's too many spirits out there. So that's what I would tell young ministers today: get in that Book and preach from the book. Study to show thyself approved.

The next thing about it is that you got to be sincere about this matter, 'cause it's just like teaching school or your profession. Your profession, you can't do anything. You got rules to go by. It's the same with the Bible; it is our rules. "I tell you the truth," Steve preached Sunday. So this is what it's all about. And that's the thing that has made me go like I did. Every place I ever went, they wanted me back. Because it's a whole lot of folks that don't even study the Bible. Call themselves preacher, and they haven't studied the Bible. And if a lot of them study it, they can't remember it. This is a God-given gift that I have.

Now, when I first started preaching in September, 1955, all right, in '60, that's when I went to Henry. Elder Pettiford started preaching for us in '56, and he preached for us ten years from '56 to '66. He would have kept on, but that Alzheimer's hit him. But when I went to that church in Henry, I told him, I said, "Elder Pettiford, I want you to anoint me with oil in my pulpit." I had just got started out preaching. He did, and I really believe that today that is why I can handle these Scriptures. Cause that's what I asked him to do; he anointed me and prayed for me right there in that pulpit. I asked for that. Because I had gotten sick of folks getting up who don't know about what the Bible had said and talking about what the Lord told them. I can go from Genesis to Revelation. I don't care who or how good they are, I can confront anybody with that Bible.

Q15: Now, we know you have the gift of playing the guitar, so kind of give us the background of how your music life started.

A15: My sister Gladys and Sugar Reeves, an old man that grew up with Papa, taught me how to play the guitar. Sugar Reeves' family was so religious, they didn't allow no guitar or drums or anything in the church back in those days. We were living right above our church now. That had to have been born in me because my daddy's folks were musicians, too. But I learned to play with him on an old guitar. We would "break a bottle" and put the neck of the bottle on this finger and use it to pick the strings of the guitar. But Gladys taught me some chords also. She could play a chord, and I played that chord, and it just started from there.

Now, Steve listens to me a lot of times. He says, "I wish I could play like that." I started playing when I was ten years old. I used to play with a bottle neck. I had an old dog named Jack. I'd take that bottle and make it go *dooo*, and he'd stand up and *whooooo*—I'd laugh. I was playing the blues then by John Henry. Yeah, my dog would be howling while I played, and I would just laugh.

Q16: Who taught you to play the piano?

A16: We had an old piano. Now, I could have been an expert pianist, but I quit playing it after I started preaching. Now, Charles could really play a piano. He could play. Now, he couldn't do much with a guitar, but he could play the piano. See, it was thirteen of us children, five of us were musicians: Nell, Hazel, Lillian, Charles, and me. Ted could blow a harmonica pretty good. Granny played the piano, too, but Papa could beat Mamma playing two to one. Papa could really play, and it sounded good. Mama told us that Uncle Roy, Uncle Robert, and Papa could play. I heard Uncle Robert play.

Now, their sister, she taught school—she and Mississippi Dobbins. They started teaching the same year. Now, when she was home she would train Papa, Uncle Roy, and Uncle Robert to make music. She would stand outside and listen to them, and if they messed up, she would come in the house and tear them up. But now Papa could play, but he would not fool with it too much after he got saved.

Q17: What advice would you give the younger generation that is coming along, pastors, or even just preachers?

A17: My advice would be to be sober, to study, never pick up or try to imitate nobody. Be who you are. Never pick up nobody's trait. I never have tried to act like somebody else. There's one little preacher that tries to be just like me; he even tries to wear his clothes like me. He said, "I want to be like Elder McBride; I want to wear my clothes like him." You see, if you try to be like that, you are not being who you are. Just be who you are. I never picked up nobody's habit, style, or nothing. I have preached all over the United States, and I don't pick up nobody's habit. I am who I am. That's the main thing—study.

Just like it was when I went to Ithaca, New York. Erma told me that somebody called her and said they didn't believe that picture was me on the program. They said that I looked too young. She asked, "Elder McBride, how old were you then?" I said, "Chiquita was two years old, so I was forty-one years old." We laughed and she said, "What they think, you have been old all of your life?" I was preaching in Ithaca, New York at that time I had that picture made. I got a letter from Cecil Malone. I didn't know him. I said now who is this? He wrote me and said, "I want you to come and run a two-week revival."

Now, your momma made me do a lot of things. So I didn't want to go. I married Charleen and Sam right there [points to the dining room entrance and laughs]. And so I read the letter. I said, "I don't know him." They had preached me at the convention. They used to preach me at the convention all the time. I would get to preach twice a year: the convention and the midwinter. They would put me up that Friday night both times. They would say, "We going to put old Mac up." That's what Bishop Young would say, "put old Mac up."

I wasn't aiming to go, but Lizzie said, "Why don't you go?" I said, "I don't know nothing about them folks," and she said, "Well go anyhow." So I got on the bus and went. So we changed buses. I wasn't that familiar with Sister Layla Robinson, but I had seen her. She was in our organization; she was James Robinson's wife. She had just left Ithaca, New York, and we changed buses, I believe, in Washington D.C. 'cause when she saw me she said, "Praise the Lord, brother." I said, "Praise the Lord." She said, "You on your way to Ithaca?" I said, "yes." She said, "I'm just coming from there, but going 'cause there is something else there to do." [He laughed.]

There was a foreigner, and he would come every night to listen to me preach. But when I got there, I didn't know they had already been running that revival for five weeks. So I didn't know that, and she was just coming from there. I said, "Lord, have mercy." Do you know Eula Payne? She's back in the P. A. of W. now. She was just a schoolgirl then. Her daddy was the deacon of the church in Ithaca, New York. They moved out of Alabama, I think when they were threatening to kill Martin Luther King. He worked at Cornell University. That big college there, that's where he worked at. A lot of those saints worked there. Anyway I was there, and that fellow would come every night; he was from Norway. Of course, when you go to New York, all kinds of nationalities are there. As he converses with his granddaughter, Trese, and her husband, Warren, he begins to tell them more about his childhood and allows them to question him on some of his spiritual beliefs.

This house here was a big old house that Mack Marshall and I tore down and rebuilt. Tilmon was the first child born in this house. An old man name Al Harris [laughs and talks about that old boy trying to build a house]. I didn't think about doing nothing like that when I was a boy. He thought that was grand for him. He thought I was foolish for building a house, but I had to stay somewhere.

When I got married, I wanted to be a husband. So when we started raising a family, I wanted to be a father for my children. I didn't want my children standing on the roadside with their noses snotty and shoes worn out. That was not the life for me. I wanted my children to have the best I could afford. Then, when I started in the ministry, I wanted to be a preacher that I could get up and preach what was in the Book. So see, that's where I'm at now, my life is fulfilled and I have met my goals and I am happy. Of course I miss your grandmomma.

Now, religion, do you not realize that religion is what drove those fellows into the towers there; that was religion. They told them that they were going to go to heaven. The Bible says, "Thou shalt not kill." See, religion will make you do crazy things, and many people have died over religion. Jim Jones had a religion, he convinced those people with that delusional spirit.

Now, going back, we went to church and school, and down here that's all we did was go to school and church. I went to the eighth grade and that's all I had for my education. When Clover Creek Baptist church started, we would go there. Then, when a new church, which was a Methodist church, would start up above Medon, we would go there. Every year we would be glad to go, and we would enjoy ourselves. But at that time, the Methodist and the Baptist didn't have fellowship. They would visit one another's church, but the Baptist would baptize once a year and the Methodists would sprinkle.

Willie Wortham was an insurance man, so he called me one evening. "Hey Reverend, I want you to go finish out my revival, my preacher go sick on me." I said, "No, you ain't doing nothing but faking." "Naw, naw, I want you to preach." I said, "You don't want me to go preach for you." So your grandmomma said, "You ought to go." I said, "He ain't doing nothing but clowning." So he carried me away to Adamsville, Tennessee to see old big Davis. He used to be at Blairs Chapel. I thought everybody knew him; he was a great big old fellow. He was a Methodist preacher, and he was already there in Adamsville preaching.

So I went there and sat down between Wortham and Davis. That was the last night of the revival, so time came for them to baptize, and they didn't do nothing but sprinkle with a pan of water. They sprinkled about sixteen people. Now, that's not even in the Bible. So they were sprinkling, and those women were shouting. One woman's daughter got baptized, oh she shouted and hollered. So ole Wortham, he was laughing and said, "We having a time tonight." I didn't say nothing. I was just sitting up in the pulpit. He looked over his shoulder at me and said, "A fellow that don't feel nothing tonight, ain't got nothing." [He laughs.]

That tickled me so bad. He was talking about me, now he got me way down there and didn't let me say a word. I was sitting up in the pulpit with them, and I said to him, "Now you see how dirty you did. Now I didn't want to come down here no how. Well, I will tell you how it was when Jesus was hanging on the cross." He said, "What is that?" I said, "I am sitting between two thieves." When I told him that, it tickled him, but it got away with him, too. And going on back to that night, I tore them up with that Bible. I told them, "Now, y'all know that it ain't a Methodist church or Baptist in this Bible, now y'all know that." They said, "Yea, yea." "Well the Bible said, blessed are the pure in heart," I said. "That's why it said that, because your heart ain't pure."

Took that little pan of water, now I said, "Baptism is a burial. You don't sprinkle. Where did you get that sprinkling at?" They said, "Well that's applied; we'll baptize and bury them if they want to." I said, "You don't do what you want to do; Jesus left us with an example." Yeah, I burned them up. But me personally, I never talked to nobody about their religion or nothing of the kind. If they don't ask me nothing, I don't tell them nothing, because in the first place you got to want to be saved. It's up to you, He [Jesus] leaves that with you. Blessed is he who hungers and thirsts after righteousness, for they shall be filled. That's Scripture, but I don't bother a man's religion.

Religion is the most powerful thing there is. There's been more killing in religion than in anything. That's what's wrong with the Muslims. They believe Muhammad was the real god. But, not so. It's like a lot of religions, they just pop up. And you can make a fool out of people, too. Yeah, you take a lot of preachers who get all of that money from all those folks, making them think that God is going to do this and God is going to do that. It's a common salvation. Salvation is a delivery from sin, that's what it is. When you repent of your sins and get baptized in Jesus's name for the remission of sin and get filled up with the Holy Ghost, then you are in the church. That is the beginning of the church. The church is in you, and you are in the church. Other than that, all these other religions are a fake. But I don't bother them, I treat people nice. I'm a person that if you need something, I'll help you.

Q18: What about the wearing of pants for women.

A18: The Bible is right, it's the true inspired Word of God. But the Bible was not written in this country. The Bible was written in the foreign countries. The people over there don't dress like we dress, no way. And so you don't make a spiritual issue out of clothes. I would have to have a biblical scripture to talk against it. Of course, there is always proper attire for any occasion. That's been a lot of our saints falling out over clothes; we got people that say you don't make an issue out of clothes. You do tell saints to dress modestly; modesty is intelligence.

Now, there are clothes for different reasons. I wouldn't go to church with a pair of shorts on, short-leg breeches and all like that. You do things decent and in order. That's what you do. You take in the foreign countries, the clothes that those people wear over there they have worn for three thousand years. The same way up until now. But yet there is a dress code in the Bible. What type of clothes they were, we really don't know. But I don't think it's nice for a person to expose their body, and I don't think it looks good coming to church with pants, but if you don't have anything but pants, that's different.

Number one, say now you got pants on and you head to the bathroom. Alright, if a man don't really know that you are a lady, he may follow you because he may think he's going to the men's room too. You see there, now that's what I'm talking about, so it's not wise to wear pants to church. A lot of people are not paying that much attention to dress attire as they used to.

Of course, when we were having all that segregation and stuff, I was traveling then. I was on my way to New York, and the bus came into Jackson. I was waiting on the bus, and a little fellow got off that bus. He didn't look at nothing whether it was men or women; he went straight into the women's bathroom. I liked to have died, it like to have given me a heart attack. [Everybody laughed.] And I said, "Lord, I hope ain't nobody in there." And it just so happened no woman was in there. They would have killed him right there on the spot. Because they were already mad anyway, he didn't pay nothing no attention, just went right into the women's bathroom.

And another thing, I read this article about a woman who was all fixed up—you know, painted up and all—and a man said something to her, and she sat him out. She told him, "I am not a harlot." He didn't say nothing until she settled down. He said, "Miss, forgive me please. If I would have known that you weren't a harlot, I never would have said anything to you, but you are dressed like one."

There are several things that can cause folks to say what they say. And you take wearing pants, yeah that's nothing new for us, not at church, we never did do that. But they always did wear pants, because our women picked cotton, so climbing up in a wagon, your dress never would have been long enough to get up there. Picking cotton, they put the pants on and then put the dress over the pants. Yea so, you got people in the organization, no doubt, they are getting better, but they don't want no pants at all. Some of them are learning better 'cause so many of the factory jobs require you to wear pants. And with some things,

41

they do look better with pants on. So they are coming to some sense on that.

Warren stated that some of the churches have a saying about come as you are, and some of us as church members are so judgmental. When you come in, you come in with your relationship with God and not the people. Bishop McBride responded: That's right. And we are working on that. Let people come as they are, but a person ought to be decent when he comes.

Trese stated that she did not understand what was wrong with wearing pants. Bishop responded: In my ministry these fifty something years, I study to maintain dignity in my church, and I don't run nobody else's church talking about pants or nothing like that. See, I know too much about the Bible to talk about pants. Some folks, they don't know nothing no how. So they just talk about things of that nature. But me personally, I don't never deal with that, because the Bible says blessed are the pure in heart, salvation makes you wise; that's Scripture. You can watch that.

Now, your grandmomma, Lizzie, didn't nobody like earrings no better than she did, and of course, down there (Marshall Chapel) you could wear earrings. So when I started in the ministry, she pulled them off herself, because a minister's wife has to be different from others. You take Chiquita; she's just fitting right in line. They can still wear earrings, little studs, but when you get something hanging way down like a dog's ear, it don't look nice to you. I mean, you may think it looks nice, but it don't. But I don't bother nothing like that.

Back in the Bible days, see the Jews first started out circumcision, came through by Abraham. That was a distinguishing mark between the Jew and the other nations. So, according to the Jews, you weren't saved if you were not circumcised. Everything that was circumcised was a Jew. Not that he was any better, but that was the distinction to know who he was. Then they had confusion in it after the church got set up. They wanted the Gentiles to be circumcised, and when they had the meeting, that's in the fifteenth chapter of Acts, they told them don't try to make the Gentiles like the Jews.

See, God gave that to Abraham to distinguish between the Jew and the Gentile; He set out a nation. That's the only thing about the Jews was that they were a special people of God, and this is how He got them like that, He circumcised them. Cornelius was the first Gentile to get saved. That's in the tenth chapter of Acts. God had to show Peter through a dream an angel of the Lord. He saw a sheet up in the air with all types of four-footed beasts and things, and that was signifying that sheet being pretty and clean and all kinds of people on there, and the Spirit says, rise Peter, slay and eat. He said, not so Lord, not anything that ever come unto me unclean. And He said, what I call clean is not unclean. So that's when Cornelius was coming to Peter then. Because Cornelius was not circumcised, and God gave Cornelius the Holy Ghost right there in front of Peter, to let him know that this man is ready for salvation just like you all. And Peter said, who can forbid water, and he baptized him in Jesus's name. This was the beginning of salvation for the Gentiles.

And they had those kinds of schemes there. In the fifteenth chapter of Acts, they had a meeting about the Jews and Gentiles, and Paul told them, don't forbid the Gentiles to live like the Jews, because the Jews had the oracles of God, they were God's chosen people. Now, there will come a time that if we all live right, we will all get together. But the church now is Jews and Gentiles. That's the church, that's the body of Christ.

The Jews are still blind to the fact, they still don't believe Jesus. They know that God was one God, that was it. They didn't know that God made Him a body Himself. Now, you go to talking to folks like that, I got the Bible for that. God prepared His own body, got in Mary's womb, and stayed nine months. I may sound like I'm talking like a fool, but that's Bible. He stayed nine months, then she birthed Him into the world. That wasn't nothing but God being made flesh. As a nation, the Jews haven't accepted that yet. And the apostles didn't know who Jesus was until He went into the hearts of the earth (ground) and stayed three days and nights and came back. Then they knew who He was. Jesus had brothers and sisters that didn't believe Him.

There's a whole lot in the Bible folks need to know. A lot of folks don't read the Bible; they don't know nothing about it. And so when the church started the day of Pentecost, the Gentiles weren't involved in that—nothing but the Jews. Every nation under heaven was there; it was the Jewish nations not the Gentiles. Cornelius was the first Gentile in the tenth chapter of Acts that received the Holy Ghost and was baptized in Jesus's name. The Bible is made up mostly from the Jews. All right, when the church leaves here, and God is controlling that—I'm not talking about a building, the church is you—it will be in midair one thousand years according to the Scriptures (found in the twentieth chapter of Revelation). He'll come back and pick up the Jews. Now, when Jesus came, He came out of Bethlehem, that's when He came here the first time. All right, when He comes back the second time to claim the Jews, He's coming out of Zion, and we don't know where that's going to be.

The Bible says the secret things belong to God, God just gives us what we are supposed to know. So that's it. I enjoy talking to folks about the Bible, but I leave it with them if they want to know about it. I don't try to make nobody believe the bible, because God is not going to make us do nothing. He says, I set before you life and death; you chose which one. What has actually gotten into people now, it's a whole lot of outside shouting. Folks just shouting who don't know nothing. After you get through shouting, you need some knowledge, you need to know how to live free from sin. Because once you get saved, you are going to lose a lot of your friends that don't believe this. And yet they expect you to fall, and they are going to try to find fault.

Everybody can know who Jesus is, if they study the Bible and obey it. They will know who He is if they will do it, but they don't want to study. I sat up until two and three o'clock in the mornings reading and studying the Bible. I read it for myself, you wouldn't know I knew anything if I didn't tell you. One sister, Sister Addie Mae, said, "You stop preaching so good when you go off, so you come back here and stay with us." But I would stay on the road all the time. People that are reading the Bible, they want to hear somebody that knows what's in the Bible.

CHAPTER SIX

LESSON PLANS FOR MINISTERS

The following are Bible classes taught by Bishop Walter McBride.

It's Your Choice

Deuteronomy 30:11-19

Psalm 118:89

St. John 10:31-33

St. John 14:8

Psalm 19:14

2 Timothy 4:1

St. Luke 24: 42-45

Psalm 58:3

Psalm 68:11

Hebrew 4:12-13

2 Timothy 3:15-17

Colossians 3:24-25

One Lord, One Faith, One Baptism

1 Timothy 1:1-11

1 John 3:16

Titus 1:10-16

1 Corinthian 3:1-3

Romans 6:16

Titus 2:1-5

The Purpose of Preaching: What Preaching Can Consist of and Who's Called to Preach

Preaching can:

1. Save You

2. Convict You

3. Condemn You

Romans 10:10-16

1 Corinthians 15:1-4

Romans 1:16

St. John 8:47

1 Corinthians 1:18-31

Hebrew 4:12-13

How to Meet God's Rules for Giving

Genesis 14:18-20

Genesis 28:22

Deuteronomy 14:22-25

Acts 2:42

Acts 4:32-35

1 Corinthians 9:7-14

Deuteronomy 23:21

Deuteronomy 14:2

St. Matthew 23:23

Acts 5:1-11

2 Peter 2:1-3

Jesus Showing His Power

St. Matthew 6:19

2 Peter 1:16-21

St. Luke 12:15-21

St. Matthew 19:26

Psalm 36:9

Ephesians 3:1-5

Ephesians 4:17-21

How to Serve God

St. Matthew 6:1-8, 30-34

1 Timothy 6:7-10

2 Corinthians 9:8-15

2 Corinthians 10:1-7

2 Corinthians 9:5-6

2 Thessalonians 3:6-11

3 John 1:1-2

1 Timothy 5:6-13

Philippians 4:13-19

Jesus Saves: What Was True Doctrine

St. Mark 16:15-20

Acts 28:1-6

Acts 4:12

St. Matthew 5:29-38

2 Timothy 3:15-16

St. Luke 24:44

St. Matthew 1:18-21

2 Corinthians 13:5

Jesus Taught Them What to Rejoice Over

St. Matthew 28:19

Ephesians 4:1-6

St. Luke 10:21-22

1 Corinthians 12:1-3

St. John 10:31

Colossians 1:23-29

Revelation 19:12-13

A Direction to Follow

Jeremiah 6:16-17

Proverbs 16:25

St. John 14:6-9

St. John 12:45-47

St. John 8:12

Isaiah 8:20

St. John 13:1-3

St. John 17:1-2

Acts 2:28-29

Acts 5:20

2 Timothy 4:1-4

2 Peter 2:1-3

St. John 8:21-24

Indoctrination

Scriptures for baptism references:
First Baptism: Crossing the Red Sea (1 Corinthians 10:1-2)
Second Baptism: John (St. Matthew 3:1-6)
Third Baptism: Day of Pentecost (Acts 4:12; St. Matthew 28:19)
The Faith (2 Corinthians 4:3-5; St. John 14:6-7; Jude 1:3)

A Complete Direction

St. Matthew 5:6-7, 20
1 Peter 2:1-2
James 3:10-17
Acts 2:5-6
Ephesians 4:17
Psalm 10:1-4

The Gospel Being Preached to Them That Believe

Hebrew 4:1-16
Isaiah 5:20; 30:8
1 Corinthians 1:14-21
1 Timothy 4:16
Romans 1:16

Be on Your Watch

2 Peter 3:1-4
2 Timothy 3:15-17
Ephesians 6:10-17
St. Luke 17:20-21
Philippians 1:20
St. Matthew 23:1

Spiritual Wisdom

Revelation 19:1-4
St. Mark 16:15-20
1 Corinthians 1:18-21
2 Peter 2:1-2
Romans 1:16; 15:11
Jeremiah 23:21-26
Colossians 3:23-25
Ephesians 4:16
Job 32:8

The Gospel: Its Benefits and How to Obtain It

Romans 1:16
Psalm 37:1-3
Ecclesiastes 8:10-13
Romans 2:1-4; 3:1-4
Proverbs 9:9-12

Spiritual Education

Zechariah 9:9
St. Matthew 21:1-5
Romans 12:14, 19-21; 16:24-26
1 Corinthians 1:1-2; 6:1-3; 15:1
2 Timothy 3:15-17
Acts 17:11; 20:32
St. Luke 24:45-47
Psalm 50:5-6
Colossians 3:24-25
Philippians 2:12
Hebrew 12:5

The Great Mystery of God

Jeremiah 10:1-12; 23:23
Ezekiel 3:1-14, 17; 12:21-28
2 Timothy 4:1
2 Peter 1:3
Romans 11:33

A Sure Foundation

Isaiah 26:9; 28:16
1 Corinthians 3:10-11
Galatians 3:27
St. Matthew 16:13-19
Ephesians 2:19
Romans 8:9; 15:26; 16:27
2 Timothy 2:19-21
St. John 16:13
Psalm 9:17
Hebrew 4:12-14
2 Corinthians 10:17-18
Acts 20:32

The Family Life

Proverbs 9:9-12; 21:23
Proverbs 26:20
James 4:11
James 3:1
James 3:10-14
Romans 12:18

Holy Ghost and the Fruit of It

1 Corinthians 12:1-6, 22-23, 26; 14:1-5, 37-40

St. John 8:24; 15:1-4, 8, 16-18

Ephesians 5:9-10

Romans 6:20

Philippians 4:15-17

Proverbs 30:6

Galatians 5:22-26

St. Matthew 7:1-16

Colossians 1:1-12

God's Authority

Psalm 135:1

Isaiah 44:24

Acts 1:8; 2:36-39

Romans 8:6-9; 11:33

Job 24:13-14

St. John 10:36; 14:16-17

St. Luke 24:44-47

1 Corinthians 6:1-4

Don't Follow What Seems Right; Follow What Is Right

Exodus 31:5

Judges 3:9-11; 6:34-35; 14:6-19

Proverbs 18:16

St. Mark 1:10

St. Luke 4:14

Romans 12:6, 8

Acts 2:1, 47

1 Peter 4:10-11

1 Corinthians 12:1

The Present Truth/ Doctrine: Who Jesus Really Is

Genesis 1:1

St. John 1:1; 4:24; 6:37-38, 58-63; 8:24; 11:31; 14:1; 17:6

"YOU DA MAN"

May 6 is when this story begins, when Walter Lewis McBride was born and raised right here in Medon, Tennessee,

The beloved son of Velma Croom and Moses McBride, born in a poor family, but managed to walk in pride,

He was the sixth child of number thirteen, and he proved early in life on whom they could depend.

He found favor with the one Elder Johnny Marshall, who saw something special in the little lad named Walter,

He went to school with his feet cold and wet, but being the smart young man he was, he figured out he could warm them by placing them inside his little hat,

His education did not go beyond eighth grade. But how would we have known that with all the accomplishments in life he's made?

He was hired out by the family to help ends meet, and regardless of what he may have suffered then, he did not suffer defeat,

At age eighteen, he married his childhood sweetheart, Lizzie Embary, who is still the most precious part of his memory.

He found himself in World War II as a very young man, where his strength and courage would be challenged once again,

We're reminded of how this man shed tears when he realized he had to be willing to kill or be killed.

He soon returned home to his wife, where Lewis was born, his first little boy. Then came Charlene their baby girl, his little bundle of joy; followed by Tilmon, Shirley, Clara, Michael, and Wayne. I know raising seven kids sometimes brought pain,

Later in life came Chiquita, to their surprise, but it didn't take long for them to see she was a jewel in disguise.

He worked long and hard as a young dad, to give his family, what he never had,

He took a job at the railroad tracks to provide a better life for his family and no turning back,

At some point in life, he saw the saints needed a church; being the man he was, even though not the pastor, he got busy and went to work.

He helped build this little church on the hill and since that time, he has never been still,

He's pastored here now for more than forty years, and I know, there has been blood, sweat, and tears.

He's instilled in the saints how to study the Word of God; to live by it and apply it to our hearts,

God has blessed Bishop McBride to know the Bible from A to Z,

And that mind of his . . . oh how amazing to me.

He's been blessed to reach age eight-four, and we all are praying for more and more and more,

He's traveled many places in this big old world with wife, Lizzie, by his side, and sometimes their little girl, so as we travel through just a small portion of his life and also remembering his darling wife.

We think of the words of President Barack Obama when we chanted, "Yes We Can!" But the saints of Whitehall Church of God say to you, "Bishop McBride, You da Man!"

Penned by
First Lady Sandra Hych
October 2010

CPSIA information can be obtained at www.ICGtesting.com
Printed in the USA
LVOW091310231111

256272LV00001B/1/P

9 781467 073066